I ordered this book for a friend in need of an anchor in the midst of a chaotic life. I was totally enthralled with it and almost sorry that I had to wrap it up and give it away. It contains a wonderful assortment of thought-provoking and uplifting quotes from sources as diverse as Albert Einstein and Henry Miller. There are also a number of beautiful examples of the watercolor work of Rod MacIver. This is a wonderful example of the potential for goodness and creativity contained in all of our diverse souls.

John Radigan

The sometimes spare, sometimes sumptuous watercolors that illustrate this little book invite you to spend time enjoying the anthology of quotes about love and gratitude. A few of the selections are short or familiar, but many are full paragraphs (or poems) and from lesser-known authors. All contribute to a mood of tranquility and appreciation — something we all need frequent doses of. Great gift for someone you love, someone you don't know well, or someone who "has everything."

Ellen N. Walker

The journey toward our beauty is a magnificent struggle. Achieving an integrity between what we believe and how we live is a challenge worthy of the gift of life. A thousand obstacles stand between ourselves and the honoring of our truth. A thousand distractions. A thousand ego-generated delusions. To dive down, find the beauty, nurture it, and offer it to the world is magnificent. Staying with your beauty, your truth, your integrity is difficult, but out of these things comes meaning, and meaning is all-transcendent.

Roderick MacIver, Artist

Your *Book of Love and Gratitude* is exceptional!!! It touched my heart in a way that is hard to express. It left me so very tearful but filled with joy & love. With Rod's art & Ann's ability to express herself & find so many beautiful quotes, it made me rejoice in "Soul Mates"... I plan to order several for friends at Christmas. Thank you for having the passion & obviously the belief in Heron Dance. You touch more people than you probably know & help to fill the journey of life with love.....

Kelly Yocum

It is a deeply reflective book which taps into several layers and angles of the human spirit, inspiring the reader to pause and listen. The watercolor images are graceful and calming, providing a soothing companion to the beautiful wisdom inside the writing. It is both a comfort and inspiration. Sitting in my rocker each night for two weeks, I turned its pages with a growing sense of peace and openness. Coaxing me into a space where I could be still and breathe, I inhaled its fresh wisdom. Now lying next to a plant by my front window, it hums a pleasant little song. Now and then I pick it up to remind myself of the importance of reflecting on life, and appreciating all its ripe beauty.

laureleaf66@hotmail.com

This book is a perfect sampling of the lovely work found on the Heron Dance website. The artwork and the poetry selections are inspirational. It is a perfect book for anyone who appreciates small forays into the aesthetic and poetic realms of language and/or watercolors.

Michelle

The *HERON DANCE* Book of
Love and Gratitude

Edited by Annie O'Shaughnessy ~ Wild Nature Paintings by Roderick MacIver

Annie O'Shaughnessy   Editor
Roderick MacIver   Artist

Hardcover
ISBN-10: 1-933937-56-4
ISBN-13: 978-1-933937-56-4

Paperback
ISBN-10: 1-933937-55-6
ISBN-13: 978-1-933937-55-7

(For an index of the paintings that appear
in this book, please go to page 82.)

Hummingbird Lane
179 Rotax Rd.
North Ferrisburg, VT 05473

www.herondance.org

Heron Dance Art Studio supports the Northeast Wilderness Trust.

Dedicated to the tender-hearted and courageous souls
who shine their light — despite everything.

In celebration of the gift of life.

Love, love, love, that is the soul of genius.

Wolfgang Amadeus Mozart

X

Introduction

I was 14 years old when I sat on the old velour couch in the dusty upstairs of our barn and wrote in my journal about love and nature. I wanted to be the next Anaïs Nin. "What do I want?" I wrote, "I want to love and explore and experience everything I can." The couch we had bought for a dollar at a tag sale smelled of spilled beer and smoke from my older siblings' parties. A layer behind that was the smell of wild creatures who had made the barn their home, and behind that the smell of coal smoke from my father's blacksmith forge on the first floor. I don't think I could have written something so naked in some spotless sitting room. This musty, dusty, dimly lit barn was perfect for dreams.

These were secret words and secret worlds, but I think back on them now as the guiding words of my life. Even at 18, when my friends and I sat around a dorm room, stoned and earnest, talking about our life goals and plans, I stuck to the same trajectory, waxing poetic about love and nature. "Love is my purpose!" I firmly stated. The talking stopped. I squirmed under their focused attention as they asked again, "No … like, what do you really want to do with your life?" Embarrassed, I tried to muster up a better, more serious response.

For years afterwards, I would ask myself the same question, over and over again. I longed for a work that I could pour my heart and soul into. The answer came when I was 34 years old, in the form of Heron Dance. Founded by Roderick MacIver in 1995, Heron Dance began as a celebration of works of love: people doing good work, people whose lives were led by love. Through his watercolors and words, it became an expression of his deep gratitude for the gift of life and his love of wild nature.

I know now that Love *is* a worthy purpose. If I could talk to my 18-year-old self, this is what I would tell her: "Live in love by availing yourself to beauty when it comes across your path; serve something greater than yourself; tell your truth to yourself over and over; surrender your old stories of fear and self-consciousness so that you can make the big space in your heart for Love to flow. Pour your heart into what you love. This is your purpose — don't let anyone or anything dissuade you."

Heron Dance asked more of me than anything else I have ever done. Many long hours working alongside Rod to keep it going burnished in me a clarity of purpose that I would not have had, had the road been easy. Heron Dance has given me countless blessings, including the privilege of assembling this book. I am deeply grateful for all of it — the good people who work there, the kind souls who support Heron Dance, and especially for Rod. Thank you.

Annie O'Shaughnessy

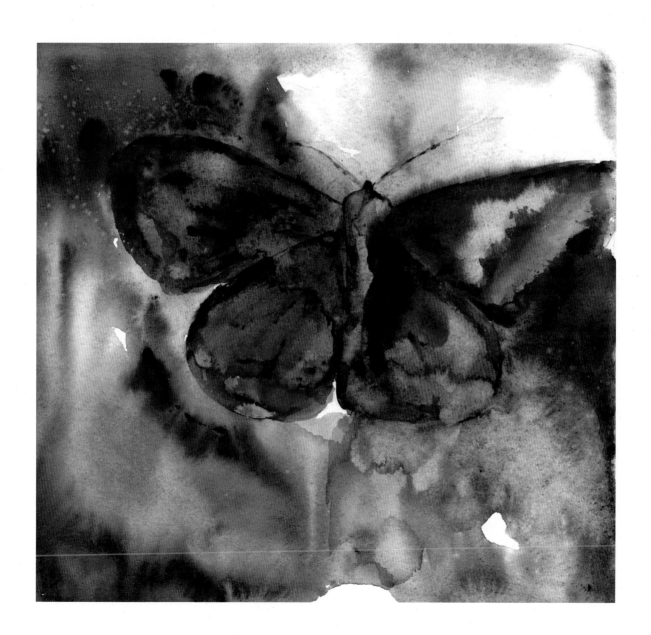

4

You will find as you look back upon your life that the moments that stand out, the moments when you have really lived, are the moments when you have done things in a spirit of love.

Henry Drummond
from *The Greatest Thing in the World*

Listen, God love everything you love — and a mess of stuff you don't.
But more than anything else, God love admiration . . . I think it pisses God off
if you walk by the color purple in a field somewhere and don't notice it.

Alice Walker from *The Color Purple*

I was lying in bed one day, thinking about my death, wondering if I'd be conscious enough to talk to my children, what I'd want to leave to them; famous last words, as it were.

The key word is trust. Trust everything that happens in life, even those experiences that cause pain will serve to better you in the end. It's easy to lose the inner vision, the greater truths, in the face of tragedy. There really is no such thing as suffering simply for the sake of suffering. Along with developing a basic trust in the rhyme and reason of life itself, I advise you to trust your intuition. It is a far better guide in the long run than your intellect.

Next on my list is to learn what love is. It is complete and utter surrender. That's a big word, surrender. It doesn't mean letting people walk all over you, take advantage of you. It's when we surrender control, let go of our egos, that all the love in the world is there waiting for us. Love is not a game, it's a state of being.

Henry Miller from *Reflections*,
edited by Twinka Thiebaud

Love all the earth, every ray of God's light, every grain of sand or blade of grass, every living thing. If you love the earth enough, you will know the divine mystery.

Fyodor Dostoevsky from *The Brothers Karamazov*

Enlightenment comes from looking at the wilderness, the creation, with eyes of awe. It is a change in perspective. Wilderness is not an enemy to be conquered, but a gift to be loved. Art [Moffatt] understood enlightenment as a "gestalt shift" in which the World is viewed differently.

What I learned from Art is that God, if there is a God, is not an object so much as a relationship — the reconciliation of all things to all things. When I feel reconciled to God, I feel awe for the gift of creation, I feel love for my fellow creatures, and I feel peace within myself. This is the gift Art shared with us.

We are very reasonable creatures, but to feel the grace of God, one must forget about reason and go on a pilgrimage to a place where we no longer "see as through a glass darkly," to a place where we are able to see the death of a caribou or a chicken with eyes of gratitude, rather than with eyes of conquest. Art had taken us on a pilgrimage to that holy place, the Garden of Eden which resides within our souls.

Jesus had spent forty days in the Wilderness, Saint Anthony a lifetime; but for us, seeing the world from a different perspective had taken about three months. It had not been until our second forty days that we had begun to feel grateful instead of angry.

Gratitude came first in the form of appreciation for small favors, small favors which we now understood to be not so small: the gift of rain, the gift of the sun, the gift of the life of a caribou which had died for us. . . . With the growing sense of gratitude came a growing sense of love: love for the creation, love for one another, and love for the grace of God which made us feel so peaceful.

> George Grinnell from *A Death on the Barrens*
> (In 1955, George Grinnell and four other young men embarked on a three-month canoe trip in Canada's Barrens led by Art Moffatt, through territory that was then largely unmapped. They ran out of food, got caught in cold weather, and Moffatt died of hypothermia when the group inadvertently went over a waterfall.)

The purpose of intimacy is to massage the heart, to soften the muscles around our hardened places and keep pliant the places where we are already open. The circle of love is deep and strong. It can forgive mistakes and cast out error. It can foster greatness and bring forth new life.

. . . This is our function in each other's lives: to hold the space for each other's beauty, that our beloved can leave us and we still feel in his (or her) absence how beautiful we are.

Marianne Williamson from *A Woman's Worth*

The things that matter most in our lives are not fantastic or grand. They are moments when we touch one another, when we are there in the most attentive or caring way. This simple and profound intimacy is the love that we all long for. These moments of touching and being touched can become a foundation for a path with heart, and they take place in the most immediate and direct way. Mother Teresa put it like this: "In this life we cannot do great things. We can only do small things with great love."

Jack Kornfield
from *A Path with Heart*

All people are wounded, but the people who come here can't cover it up the way the rest of us do. Everybody has pain, everybody is wounded. And because the [Commonweal retreat] participants can't cover up their woundedness now that they have cancer, they can trust each other. I can trust another person only if I can sense that they, too, have woundedness, have pain, have fear.

[When you have cancer] you feel separated from the whole human race. You feel as though you're looking at the world through plate glass. You can see other people, but you feel as if you can't touch them or be with them, because you are different. They say that the sense of isolation, of being separated from people who are well, is as painful as chemotherapy, as cancer itself. . . .

Years ago, when I was Associate Director of the pediatric clinics at the Stanford Medical School, one of my colleagues, Marshall Klaus, did a study which at the time was extremely innovative. He was chief of the intensive care nursery, where all the babies were these tiny little people you could hold in your hand. Each incubator was surrounded by shifts of people and millions of dollars worth of equipment. Everything was high-tech. Of course, we didn't touch these infants because we'd get germs on them. But Klaus decided to do an experiment in which half the babies in the nursery would be treated as usual, and the other half would be touched for fifteen minutes every few hours. You'd take your pinky finger and rub it down the little baby's back. And we discovered that the babies that were touched survived better. No one knows why. Maybe there's something about touching that strengthens the will to live. Maybe isolation weakens us.

Rachel Naomi Remen, Cofounder of the Commonweal Cancer Help Program, as interviewed by Bill Moyers in *Healing and the Mind*

Love has nothing to do with what you are expecting to get — only what you are expecting to give — which is everything. What you will receive in return varies. But really has no connection with what you give. You give because you love and cannot help giving. If you are very lucky, you may get loved back. That is delicious, but it does not necessarily happen.

    Katharine Hepburn

Jnani talks to the body as she works on it, and she talks especially to wounds. She coaxes wounded bodies and spirits out of pain and tension and into relaxation and a new peace. People who have associated being touched with pain, as they have been cut and injected and radiated and saturated with chemotherapy, now experience some of the most healing touch of their lives. People who have not been touched with love in many years experience what it is to be touched again with love. . . . I remember the evening we talked about death and dying at a Smith Farm Cancer Help Program when a very young woman with metastatic breast cancer, married to a carpenter, with a three-year-old daughter, began to shake uncontrollably at the end of the evening. Jnani was stroking her, whispering to her, coaxing her through the psychic pain that had taken over her body. Jnani brought her back to peace.

Michael Lerner, President of the Commonweal
Cancer Help Program, from its newsletter

"*You don't know*, or maybe you do," said Mr. Hal, a look of deep satisfaction with the coffee and with his thoughts on his face, "how wonderful a feeling it give you when you know somebody love you and that's just the way it is. You can be a devil, and still that somebody love you. You can be weak, you can be strong; you can know a heap or nearly nothing. That kind of love, when you think about it, just seems like some kind of puzzle, and you can spend your whole lifetime trying to figure it out. If you puffed up with vanity, you can't help but think that they is something you created yourself. Or maybe it your money or your car. But there's something. . . . It's like how you love a certain place. You just do that's all. And if you are lucky, while you're on this earth, you get to visit it. And the place 'knows' about your love. That was the love and still is the love between Lissie and me."

Alice Walker from *The Temple of My Familiar*

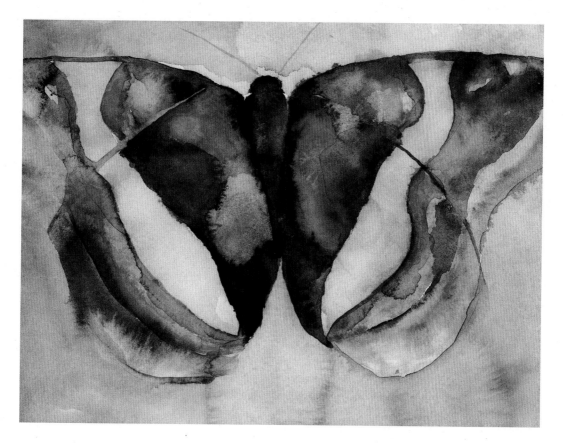

God changes appearances every second. Blessed is the man who can recognize him in all his disguises. One moment he is a glass of fresh water, the next, your son bouncing on your knees or an enchanting woman, or perhaps merely a morning walk.

Nikos Kazantzakis

I had wondered why within Findhorn there was the absolute absence of dogma and proselytization. I knew then that it was because there was nothing to preach, nothing to defend, nothing to hold on to. At Findhorn, people don't talk about planetary service, yet they demonstrate it in their everyday life by emptying ash bins and selling potatoes in the shop. It is not what they do — it is the manner in which everything is done. It is the extraordinary care, love, and dedication that you see in Don taking care of a patron at the store, or in Richard when he pours a concrete slab, or in Joanie when she counts the sheets and towels, or in all the people living their daily lives, serving the whole, knowing that God and they are one.

Paul Hawken from *The Magic of Findhorn*

From the age of six to fourteen I took violin lessons but had no luck with my teachers, for whom music did not transcend mechanical practicing. I really began to learn only after I had fallen in love with Mozart's sonatas. The attempt to reproduce their singular grace compelled me to improve my technique. I believe, on the whole, that love is a better teacher than sense of duty.

Albert Einstein

Some say the creative life is in ideas, some say it is in doing. It seems in most instances to be in simply being. It is not virtuosity, although that is very fine in itself. It is the love of something, having so much love for something — whether a person, a word, an image, an idea, the land, or humanity — that all that can be done with the overflow is to create. It is not a matter of wanting to, not a singular act of will; one solely must.

Clarissa Pinkola Estés from *Women who Run with the Wolves*

The mind I love must still have
wild places, a tangled orchard where the
dark damsons drop in the heavy grass,
an overgrown little woods, the chance of
a snake or two (real snakes), a pool that
nobody's fathomed the depth of — and
paths threaded with those little flowers
planted by the mind.

Katherine Mansfield

I have come to believe that most of us have experienced some lonely spot, some private nook, some glen or streamside-scene that impressed us so deeply that even today its memory recalls the mood of a lost enchantment. At the age of eighty, my grandmother used to recall with delight a lonely tract she called "Beautiful Big South Woods." There, as a girl one spring day, she had seen the whole floor of the woods, acre on acre, carpeted with the blooms of bloodroot and spring beauties and blue and pink hepaticas. She had seen the woods only once but she never forgot it.

Edwin Way Teale from *The Lost Woods*

The Mother's Song

It is so still in the house.
There is a calm in the house;
The snowstorm wails out there,
And the dogs are rolled up with snouts under the tail.
My little boy is sleeping on the ledge,
On his back he lies, breathing through his open mouth.
His little stomach is bulging round —
Is it strange if I start to cry with joy?

Inuit Song, as recorded by Knud Rasmussen

It was time to feed the horses. I decided to take advantage of the opportunity to lie down in the shade of a big cedar, and dropped off to sleep at once. In a couple of hours Olentiev awakened me and I looked around. I saw Dersu splitting firewood and collecting birch bark and stacking it all in the hut.

I thought at first that he wanted to burn it down, and started dissuading him from the idea. Instead of replying, he asked me for a pinch of salt and a handful of rice. I was interested to see what he was going to do with it, so told the men to give him some. The Gold carefully rolled up some matches in birch bark, and the salt and rice, each separately, in rolls of birch bark, and hung it all inside the hut. He then started packing his own things.

"You'll probably be coming back here one of these days, I suppose?" I asked him.

He shook his head, so I then asked him for whom he was leaving the matches, salt, and rice.

"Some other man, he come," answered Dersu, "He find dry wood, he find matches, he find food, not die."

I well remember how struck I was by this. It was wonderful, I thought, that the Gold should bother his head about an unknown man whom he never would see, and who would never know who had left him the provisions. I thought how my men, on leaving a bivouac, always burnt up all the bark left at the fire. They did it out of no ill-will, but simply for amusement, to see the blaze, and I never used to stop them from doing so. And here was this savage far more thoughtful for others than I.

V.K. Arseniev from *Dersu the Trapper*

...that best portion of a good man's life,
His little, nameless, unremembered acts
Of kindness and of love.

William Wordsworth

The boat I travel in is called Surrender. My two oars are instant forgiveness and gratitude — complete gratitude for the gift of life. I am thankful for the experience of this life, for the opportunity to dance. I get angry, I get mad, but as soon as I remind myself to put my oars in the water, I forgive.

I serve. I do the dance I must. I plant trees, but I am not the doer of this work. I am the facilitator, the instrument — I am one part of the symphony. I know there is an overall scheme to this symphony that I cannot understand. In some way, we are each playing our own part. It is not for me to judge or criticize the life or work of another. All I know is that this is my dance. I would plant trees today even if I knew for certain that the world would end tomorrow.

Balbir Mathur, founder of Trees for Life,
from a *Heron Dance* interview, Issue 11

In music, in a flower, in a leaf, in an act of kindness. . .
I see what people call God in all these things.

Pablo Casals

I think that those who serve most potently work on
levels of consciousness that have to do with radiating love —
maybe God's love. My own experience is that people who
work with love operate on some level deeper than the
conscious. It is important that you have a brain and use
it, but that is secondary. The basic premise is that you
allow something to come through you. Then you use your
intelligence to give your work form, to give your heart's
work discipline and logic. But the transformative energy,
that which can change events, that heals, that helps, that
serves, comes from somewhere deep inside.

Julie Glover from a *Heron Dance* interview, Issue 1

As we love ourselves, we move toward our own bliss, by which Joseph Campbell meant our highest enthusiasm. The word "entheos" means "god-filled." Moving towards that which fills us with the godhood, that place where time is not, is all we need to do to change the world around us. Then we, naturally and without effort, love others and allow them to move beyond their self-imposed limitations, and in their own ways. The goal is to evolve to that place where the energy that had been projected outward to correct the world is turned around to correct oneself — to get on our own track and to dance, in balance, between the worlds.

Following your bliss, as Joseph meant it, is not self-indulgent but vital; your whole physical system knows that this is the way to be alive in this world and the way to give the world the very best that you have to offer. There is a track just waiting for each of us, and once on it, doors will open that were not open before and would not open for anyone else. Everything does start clicking along, and yes, even Mother Nature herself supports the journey.

I have found that you have only to take that one step toward the gods and they will then take ten steps toward you. That step, the heroic first step of the journey, is out of, or over the edge of, your boundaries, and it often must be taken before you know that you will be supported. The hero's journey has been compared to a birth; it starts out warm and snug in a safe place; then comes a signal, growing more insistent, that it is time to leave. To stay beyond your time is to putrefy. Without the blood and tearing and pain, there is no new life.

Joseph Campbell from *A Joseph Campbell Companion*,
selected and edited by Diane K. Osbon

i found god in myself
& I loved her
i loved her fiercely

Ntozake Shange

I have come to know simple truths that before were disguised by my complexity. I have come to know the inner vision that sees with much clarity. I've come to know me, the gentleness of my spirit, as it may express itself through love and tenderness. I've come to know power in a way that's personal and creative. My personal power of choice. I've come to know love; love of self and others is the same. I've come to know the oneness of all who walk the planet in an attempt to journey home.

Greta Metcalf

After a life of so much wandering and looking and hoping for meaning in people, places and circumstances outside myself, I grabbed the essentials and dove inward. It has been, and continues to be, a slow, often bewildering trip, consisting of many baby steps on wobbly legs. Speaking my truth or hearing another's truth still makes my heart pound in my chest. But what I keep discovering is that truth coupled with love and grace has a magical quality — creating doors where there were only walls and providing light on a path once hidden. A light so bright I can see it even as I drift from the known — untethered and a little afraid — into the unknown.

Ann O'Shaughnessy from Heron Dance's
weekly email *A Pause for Beauty*

If you listen,
not to the pages or preachers
but to the smallest flower
growing from a crack
in your heart,
you will hear a great song
moving across a wide ocean
whose water is the music
connecting all the islands
of the universe together,
and touching all
you will feel it
touching you
around you. . .
embracing you
with light.

It is in that light
that everything lives
and will always be alive.

John Squadra from *This Ecstasy*

I went off with fists
In my torn pockets;
My coat was completely
Threadbare.
I followed you, Muse,
Where you led me,
Dreamed of loves —
Ah — so fine and so rare.

      Rimbaud from
      the poem "Ma Boheme"

It is not pleasant to feel that friends who have loved us no longer care for us. One says defiantly, "I don't care! I am perfectly happy without their friendship;" but it is not true. One cannot help feeling very sad about it at times. We are all complex. I wish I were made of just one self — consistent, wise, and loving — a self I should never wish to get rid of at any time or place, which would move graciously through my autobiography, "trailing clouds of glory." But alas and alack! Deep within me I knew nothing of the kind would happen. No wonder I shrank from writing this book.

It is no use trying to reconcile the multitude of egos that compose me. I cannot fathom them myself. I ask myself questions that I cannot answer. I find my heart aching when I expected to find it rejoicing, tears flow from my eyes when my lips were formed to smile. I preach love, brotherhood, and peace, but I am conscious of antagonisms, and lo! I find myself brandishing a sword and making ready for battle.

. . . I believe in the immortality of the soul because I have within me immortal longings. I believe that the state we enter after death is wrought of our own motives, thoughts, and deeds. I believe that in the life to come I shall have the senses I have not had here, and that my home there will be beautiful with color, music, speech of flowers and faces I love.

Without this faith there would be little meaning in my life. I should be "a mere pillar of darkness in the dark." Observers in the full enjoyment of their bodily senses pity me, but it is because they do not see the golden chamber in my life where I dwell delighted; for, dark as my path may seem to them, I carry a magic light in my heart. Faith, the spiritual strong searchlight, illumines the way, and although sinister doubts lurk in the shadow, I walk unafraid towards the Enchanted Wood where the foliage is always green, where joy abides, where nightingales nest and sing, and where life and death are one in the Presence of the Lord.

Helen Keller from *Midstream, My Later Life*

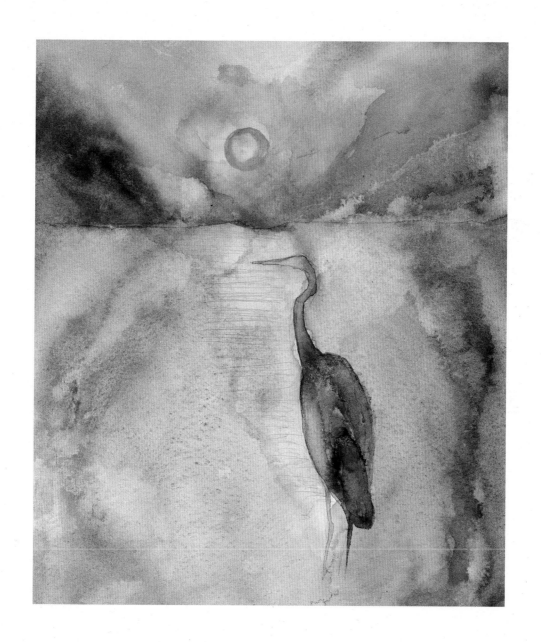

Surrender to love is the hardest damn work I have ever done in my life. Put me working in prisons to teach murderers how to give good massages or give me women who haven't slept without nightmares in ten years, but don't ask me to be open and receive tender loving care from someone who is going to know all my dirty laundry and stick around anyway!

Why is it so hard? Well, I guess I've just been on the road so long I don't know the difference between my feet and my boots, and then here comes someone to offer a foot rub and I gotta feel how tired my feet are and how long I've been wanting some good touch and lay down all those other times of disappointment and confusion, and let this in without overwhelming myself, or anyone else, with grief and longing. I didn't learn how to do this at home or school. Did you? It takes a combination of mercy and love we give ourselves.

John Calvi from "True Love," *The Friends Journal*, 1992

For the world is not painted or adorned, but is from the beginning beautiful; and God has not made some beautiful things, but Beauty is the creator of the universe.

Ralph Waldo Emerson

The transition from tenseness, self-responsibility, and worry, to equanimity, receptivity, and peace, is the most wonderful of all those shiftings of inner equilibrium, those changes of the personal center of energy, which I have analyzed so often; and the chief wonder of it is that it so often comes about, not by doing, but by simply relaxing and throwing the burden down.

William James

Last night when I cycled home from S., I poured out all my tenderness, all the tenderness one cannot express for a man even when one loves him very, very much, I poured it all out into the great, all-embracing spring night. I stood on the little bridge and looked across the water; I melted into the landscape and offered all my tenderness up to the sky and the stars and the water and to the little bridge. And that was the best moment of the day.

. . . And I felt this was the only way of transforming all the many deep and tender feelings one carries for another into deeds: to entrust them to nature, to let them stream out under the open spring sky, and to realize that there is no other way of letting them go.

Etty Hillesum from *An Interrupted Life*

Oh, Earth, you're too wonderful
for anybody to realize you.

Thornton Wilder

The world is rude, silent, incomprehensible at first,
nature is incomprehensible at first.
Be not discouraged, keep on,
there are divine things well envelop'd,
I swear to you there are divine beings
more beautiful than words can tell.

     Walt Whitman

Love is the fruit of beauty. When you see a beautiful tree, you fall in love — ah, beautiful flowers, the bluebells, the primroses! Beauty enters the heart and creates love. That is why in the world today we lack love, because there is less and less beauty in our everyday lives. Whenever you make something with love, you feel humbled. You could not make such beautiful things on your own. It must come through divine inspiration. In that way, beauty and humility go together. It is an act of surrender to the divine source. The divine inspiration uses your body, your hands, and your talents, as a channel for beauty, whether it is a Henry Moore sculpture or a painting by Van Gogh or some beautiful peasant house in rural Vermont. Or beautiful shoes made in Rajistan. . . . Therefore beauty is a source of spiritual healing. For me, beauty is the essence of our being, the soul of our being.

Satish Kumar from a
Heron Dance interview, Issue 23

What lifts the heron leaning on the air
I praise without a name. A crouch, a flare,
a long stroke through the cumulus of trees,
a shaped thought at the sky — then gone. O rare!
Saint Francis, being happiest on his knees,
would have cried Father! Cry anything you please

But praise. By any name or none. But praise
the white original burst that lights
the heron on his two soft kissing kites.
When saints praise heaven lit by doves and rays,
I sit by pond scums till the air recites
Its heron back. And doubt all else. But praise.

John Ciardi from *The White Heron*

*The following poem was sent in by a subscriber who enclosed the note
"read it aloud three times — you'll 'feel' it land on your pond."*

Flowers unfold slowly and gently, bit by bit in the sunshine, and a soul too must never be punished or driven, but unfolds in its own perfect timing to reveal its true wonder and beauty.

The Findhorn Community from *The Findhorn Garden*

I believe that God is in me as the sun is in the color and fragrance of a flower — the Light in my darkness, the Voice in my silence.

Helen Keller

Near the end of the war, he was injured in an explosion which seriously impaired his vision. Told that his loss of sight would eventually be total, he decided to return to more familiar surroundings in France to continue his study of music and to prepare himself to leave the world of the sighted. "The sight of a pin," he wrote, "a hair, a leaf, a glass of water—these filled me with tremendous excitement. The plants in the courtyards, the cobblestones, the lamp posts, the faces of strangers. I no longer took them in and bound them up in me, they retained their values, their identities. I went out to them, immersed myself in them and found them more beautiful than I ever dreamed they could be. They taught, they nourished when one gave oneself to them."

Robert Ellsberg from a profile of John Howard Griffin
in *The Catholic Worker*

Silent wings slowly
Low above waters of a misty morning lake
Teaching me tranquility

Steve Braun

I remember paddling in the Baja, through some perfectly smooth, jade green water. On the bottom were sea cucumbers, rock scallops, some beautiful seaweeds. Everybody started to go very slow. We had been paddling hard, but everybody slowed down and just started looking. After about fifteen minutes of quiet, we picked up our paddles and started paddling again. There was so much power in that silence, that the next day we did the whole day without talking. In silence there is a lot more access, I think, to the spirit, to spirituality, to the soul.

Jennifer Hahn from a *Heron Dance* interview, Issue 1

Moved

The great sea stirs me.
The great sea sets me adrift,
it sways me like the weed
on a river-stone.

The sky's height stirs me.
The strong wind blows through my mind.
It carries me with it,
and moves my inner parts with joy.

       Uvanuk, woman shaman of the Igloolik Inuit,
       as recorded by Knud Rasmussen

One July afternoon at our ranch in the Canadian Rockies, I rode toward Helen Keller's cabin. Along the wagon trail that ran through a lovely wood we had stretched a wire, to guide Helen when she walked there alone, and as I turned down the trail I saw her coming.

I sat motionless while this woman, who was doomed to live forever in a black and silent prison, made her way briskly down the path, her face radiant. She stepped out of the woods into a sunlit open space directly in front of me and stopped by a clump of wolf willows. Gathering a handful, she breathed their strange fragrance: her sightless eyes looked up squarely into the sun, and her lips, so magically trained, pronounced the single word "Beautiful!" Then, still smiling, she walked past me.

I brushed the tears from my own inadequate eyes. For to me, none of this exquisite highland had seemed beautiful. I had felt only bitter discouragement over the rejection of a piece of writing. I had eyes to see all the wonders of woods, sky, and mountains, ears to hear the rushing stream and the song of the wind in the treetops. It took the sightless eyes and sealed ears of this extraordinary woman to show me beauty and bravery.

Frazier Hunt from *Redbook* magazine

Make me an instrument of thy peace
Where there is hatred, let me sow love
Where there is doubt, faith
Where there is despair, hope
Where there is darkness, light
Where there is sadness, joy.

Grant that I may not so much seek
To be consoled as to console
To be understood as to understand
To be loved as to love
For it is in giving that we receive
It is in pardoning that we are pardoned
It is in dying that we are born to eternal life.

The Ancient Prayer of St. Francis

Let us keep this truth before us. You say you have no faith? Love — and faith will come. You say you are sad? Love — and joy will come. You say you are alone? Love — and you will break out of your solitude. You say you are in hell? Love — and you will find yourself in heaven. Heaven is love.

Carlo Carretto
from *In Search of the Beyond*

Your life will have a kind of perfection, although you will not be a saint. The perfection will consist in this: you will be very weak and you will make many mistakes; you will be awkward, for you will be poor in spirit and hunger and thirst for justice. You will not be perfect, but you will love. This is the gate and the way. There is nothing greater than love. There is nothing more true than love, nothing more real. So let us hand our lives over to love and seal the bond of love.

Eberhard Arnold from *The Daily Dig*

The Gate

No one compels you, traveler;
this road or that road, make your choice!
Dust or mud, heat or cold,
fellowship or solitude,
foul weather or a fairer sky,
the choice is yours as you go by.

But here if you would take this path
there is a gate whose latch is love,
whose key is single and which swings
upon the hinge of faithfulness,

and none can mock, who seeks this way,
the king we worship shamelessly.
If you would enter, traveller,
into this city fair and wide,
it is forever and you leave
all trappings of the self outside.

Jane Tyson Clement

4 a.m. in Katmandu

It's 4 a.m. in Katmandu
I lie awake in the silent room
I hear my lady stir and rise
she comes and lays close by my side.

I turn and gather her to me
and gently ravish every crease
we feel our love ignite and leap
and give ourselves to grateful heat

    and afterwards the birds
    the sparrows stir
    and the pigeons land
    on the corrugated roof
    in a mating dance
    and then fly off
    like fan belts chirping
    and the roosters crow
    and the dogs are barking
    and we're aglow

And we are so full
we are so full
the world is so full
our lives are so full!

My arm across her lovingly
shares the warmth of her body
with the coolness of the morning air
and we're basking in this moment rare

    and the kitchens crackle
    in the streets below
    and the rickshaws rattle
    on the cobblestone
    and the sun slips down
    the undulating wall
    and the awareness dawns
    that we have it all

Will Danforth from his album
Grey Dawn Breaking

Do you not see
That you and I
Are as the branches of one tree?
With your rejoicing
Comes my laughter;
With your sadness
Start my tears
Love,
Could life be otherwise
With you and me?

       Tsu Yeh, AD 265–316

We die containing a richness of lovers and tribes, tastes we have swallowed, bodies we have plunged into and swum up as if rivers of wisdom, characters we have climbed into as if trees, fears we have hidden in as if caves. I wish for all this to be marked on my body when I am dead, I believe in such cartography — to be marked by nature, not just to label ourselves on a map like the names of rich men and women on buildings. We are communal histories, communal books. We are not owned or monogamous in our taste of experiences. All I desired was to walk upon such an earth that had no maps.

Michael Ondaatje from *The English Patient*

To love means never to be afraid of the windstorms of life: should you shield the canyons from the windstorms you would never see the true beauty of their carvings.

Elisabeth Kübler-Ross, M.D.

But authenticity, and this beauty, includes brokenness and darkness and death. In moments of darkness and uncertainty, we encounter the depths of our desire that life go on. And, paradoxically, it opens us up to gratitude for this moment — our chance to breathe the air, feel our heart beating, look into the eyes of another being. In times like that, what's trivial or tawdry gets stripped away. And the stark grandeur appears. A grandeur that reaches down into our hearts.

JoAnna Macy from a *Heron Dance* interview, Issue 23

The whole thing in marriage is the relationship and yielding. Marriage is not a love affair. A love affair has to do with immediate personal satisfaction. Marriage is an ordeal; it means yielding, time and again. That's why it is a sacrament: you give up your personal simplicity to participate. And you are not giving to the other person; you are giving to the relationship. Because you are not giving to the other person, it is not impoverishing — it is life building, life fostering, enriching.

. . . The beautiful thing is the growing: each helping the other to flower. We often want to freeze the other person, but you can't have that and love too.

Joseph Campbell from *A Joseph Campbell Companion*, selected and edited by Diane K. Osbon

So much of the satisfaction in life is in taking a risk for the thing you love.

Rod MacIver from a *Heron Dance* interview

When you love,
you complete a circle.

When you die,
the circle remains.

John Squadra from *This Ecstasy*

In Greek mythology Eros was the son of Aphrodite, the Goddess of Love. The term "eros" represents the creative force of highly spiritual, sexual yearning or love. C.G. Jung said, "people think that eros is sex, but not at all, eros is relatedness." Eros represents the spiritual, emotional and the physical aspects of sex combined. It is the intense bond created by the involved couples. Plato writes: "Eros is a coming to life in beauty in relation to both body and soul."

Debora Myer from *An Erotic Life*

In our society, we've become myopic and obsessive with one particular kind of love: dyadic love, which takes the form of romance, sex, marriage. As a result we end up asking all the wrong questions. Books about relationships talk about how to "get" the love you need, how to "keep" love, and so on. But the right question to ask is: "How do I become a more loving human being?" When you ask that question, it changes the way you think about pursuing love, making it much more complex.

Sam Keene from *The Sun Magazine*

Out beyond ideas of wrong-doing and right-doing,
there is a field. I'll meet you there.

When the soul lies down in that grass,
the world is too full to talk about.
Ideas, language, even the phrase "each other" doesn't make any sense.

Jalal ad-Din Rumi

Always say what you feel, and do what you think is good and
right. If I knew that today would be the last time I'd see you, I would
hug you tight and pray the Lord be the keeper of your soul. If I knew
that this would be the last time you pass through this door, I'd embrace
you, kiss you, and call you back for one more. If I knew that this would
be the last time I would hear your voice, I'd take hold of each word to
be able to hear it over and over again. If I knew this is the last time I'd
see you, I'd tell you I love you, and would not just assume foolishly you
know it already.

Gabriel García Márquez

the best lover ever

the best lover ever
was a czechoslovakian, macrobiotic
cardiac surgeon who carried viburnum
flowers in from the garden to lay
them on my belly before pressing
them flat and fragrant with his own.

reaching above the bed for the stethoscope
that hung there, he laid the cool, flat
membrane against my neck, below the
ridge of my clavicle, along the
margins of my breast, listening to all
the chambers, portals, and vessels
of my heart.

(ah, the pleasure of lying naked
before a man who undresses you
further still.)

the good doctor, at the end of his
exploration, pronounced with a certainty
that resonates still: "you haf a gud heart."

now, the wise among you already
know the end of this story.

the czechoslovakian, macrobiotic
cardiac surgeon, the best lover ever,
followed his books
back to the homeland to listen to
other hearts, bear a few children,
have a dog named bonnie.

perhaps you know I married a man
far less kind, who took that same
heart and pried it open with the
crowbar of his own great
disappointment.

can you tell me, does it matter to
the heart who opens it?
does it matter to the heart whether
it is cleaved with force or tenderness?

and is the light any less pleased,
any less persistent as it streams
through the fissures, finally
illuminating the interior?

Lillian Ralph Jackman,
June 1999

So now I was in the Hole for the first time, no light, no bed, shivering in the midst of summer in a cell that was damper and darker than the Swiss dungeon of Chillon that Byron had written about and that I had visited a couple of years earlier. "You won't come out," they had said, "until you agree to obey orders, all orders.". . .

For no reason I can explain, I began to discover how little it mattered where you are or what anyone does to you. I was sure that what I had done to get there was right and somehow the longer I was there the better I felt. . . . I felt warm inside and filled all over with love for everyone, everyone I knew and everyone I didn't know, for plants, for fish, animals, even bankers, generals, prison guards and lying politicians — everything and everyone. Why did I feel so good? Was it God? Or approaching death? Or just the way life is supposed to be if we weren't so busy trying to make it something else?

. . . From now on, no one will ever frighten or control me, no one will stop me from living to the full and loving to the full, loving everyone I know and everyone I don't know, fighting for justice without seeing anyone as an enemy.

David Dellinger from *Yale to Jail*

So here's what I wanted to tell you today: Get a life: a real life, not a manic pursuit of the next promotion, the bigger paycheck, the larger house. Do you think you'd care so very much about those things if you blew an aneurysm one afternoon, or found a lump in your breast? Get a life in which you notice the smell of salt water pushing itself on a breeze over Seaside Heights, a life in which you stop and watch how a red-tailed hawk circles over the water or the way a baby scowls with concentration when she tries to pick up a Cheerio with her thumb and first finger. Get a life in which you are not alone. Find people you love, and who love you.

. . . I found one of my best teachers on the boardwalk at Coney Island maybe 15 years ago. It was December, and I was doing a story about how the homeless survive in the winter months. He and I sat on the edge of the wooden supports, dangling our feet over the side, and he told me about his schedule, panhandling the boulevard when the summer crowds were gone, sleeping in a church when the temperature went below freezing, hiding from the police amidst the Tilt-a-Whirl and the Cyclone, and some of the other seasonal rides. But he told me that most of the time he stayed on the boardwalk, facing the water, just the way we were sitting now, even when it got cold and he had to wear his newspapers after he read them. And I asked him why. Why didn't he go to one of the shelters? Why didn't he check himself into the hospital for detox? And he just stared out at the ocean and said, "Look at the view, young lady. Look at the view."

And every day, in some little way, I try to do what he said. I try to look at the view. And that is the last thing I have to tell you today, words of wisdom from a man with not a dime in his pocket, no place to go, nowhere to be. Look at the view. You'll never be disappointed.

Anna Quindlen from her commencement address
at Villanova University, February 8, 1999

If of thy mortal goods thou art bereft
and of thy store two loaves are left
sell one, and with the dole
buy hyacinths to feed thy soul

Sa'di, AD 1248

The true source of joy is love —
love of God, love of beauty, love
of wisdom, love of another human
being, it does not matter which. It
is all one love: a joyful awareness
of dissolving boundaries of our
ordinary narrow self, of being one
with the reality beyond, of being
made whole.

Irma Zaleski
from *The Door to Joy*

Most of All, They Taught Me Happiness
by Dr. Robert Muller

Love for life, passion for life, deep gratitude for every moment of it, extending one's heart and brain into eternity and totality, from the fishes and the fowl to the stars, from youth to old age, from the glaciers to the tropics, from the prodigy of birth to the mystery of death, man can indeed partake in all creation if he switches on, deep inside, the will for life, the decision for happiness, the option for love. I have "decided" to love my life, to throw in my gauntlet for it, to believe in it, to find it exalting in every respect, at every moment, from the beginning to the end. . . .

. . . There is so much magic in life, in these colors, in these shapes, in this drop of shining light in the gigantic dark universe. Yes, our planet is a prodigious miracle, a unique happening in billions of years of evolution, in aeons of light years of space. We will never cherish it enough. We will never be grateful enough. This miracle should be the object of our constant love, joy, and admiration. We should stand in awe before the mysterious forces that brought it into being. But instead, so many of us are complaining, unhappy, and somber. How is that possible? Why can't we realize that all this could well not be, that evolution could have produced a different planet, a lifeless planet, at another distance from the sun, with a different inclination or orbit, a different atmosphere, flora, and fauna, another human body, heart, and mind? All great religions, prophets, and visionaries saw it better than the scientists of today. They demanded respect for creation and for the mysterious forces behind it. Our colossal contemporary knowledge should have increased our elation and our thankfulness for the wonders of nature. Instead, we have lost much of our love and happiness. We must lift ourselves again high above our microscopes, telescopes, books, newspapers, and computers, and see again the total beauty of a flower, of a brook, of a woman, of a child, of the world, of the stars.

Yes, our miraculous planet Earth should irradiate human thankfulness and joy into every direction of the universe.

Love is the only way out, the secret of secrets. Happiness is a state of mind, a click inside us, a conscious, determined decision or will to embrace with fascination, enthusiasm (that is, by God possessed), the entire world and creation. Happiness is total consciousness. Happiness is the peak fulfillment of life. It is a human's own doing, his greatest power and liberty. Happiness is not external to man, it is a genial force in him. It cannot be elsewhere. It is not part of nature or of the world, it is an attribute, an essence of the human person. It is above prison, death, poverty, disability, injustice, age, inequality, and prejudice.

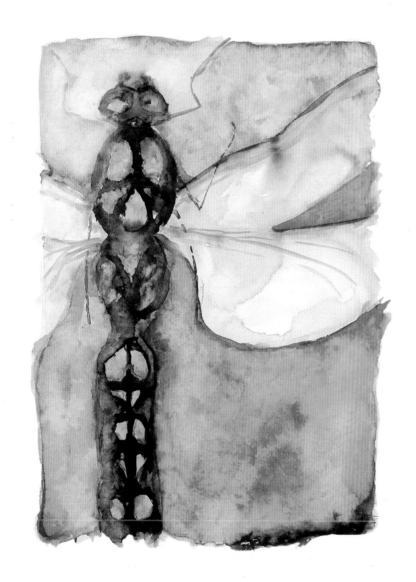

73

A vagabond in a ditch, a deprived artist or poet, an invalid, an uneducated tribesman surrounded by his wife and children can be a thousand times happier than an insatiable, neurotic millionaire in his skyscraper. Billions of happy humans have walked on this planet throughout the ages who did not have the blessings of today. Happiness is the great revanche of the poor, the dreamers, the poets, the artists, the visionaries, the simple, the wise, the diminished, and all those guided by the heart rather than by power, money, and interest. Happiness is increasingly vital in a world of growing numbers, complexity, and anonymity, where glory is becoming increasingly difficult.

. . . When the moment will come to close my eyes on this beautiful planet, my heart will thank and honor all those who gave me life and the warmth of love, and Him who permitted me to devote my earthly sojourn to peace, justice, and the betterment of the human condition in the United Nations — one of the noblest organizations ever born from the heart of man. I will go in peace and joy, thankful for having been blessed with the miracle of life.

I will have loved my life with passion, embraced it with fervor, cherished every single moment of it. I will have contemplated with wonder the sky and its running clouds, my brethren the humans, my sisters the flowers and stars. I will have feasted unceasingly on the treasure of life in all its forms. I will not have dwelled in mediocre ambitions, vain hatred, and useless complaints.

I will depart with the belief that there is no end to the flow of life in the universe, that there is no death but only an unceasing change of worlds.

My conclusion would therefore be:

decide to be happy

render others happy

proclaim your joy

love passionately your miraculous life

do not listen to promises

do not wait for a better world

be grateful for every moment of life

switch on and keep on the positive buttons in yourself,

those marked optimism, serenity, confidence, positive thinking, love

pray and thank God every day

meditate

smile

laugh

whistle

sing

dance

look with fascination at everything

fill your lungs and heart with liberty

be yourself fully and immensely

act like a king unto Death

feel God in your body, mind, heart, and soul

and be convinced of eternal life and resurrection.

God bless you,

Robert Muller

A PAUSE FOR BEAUTY
The HERON DANCE E-Newsletter

Each free e-newsletter features Roderick MacIver's latest wild nature painting, selected quotes from poetry and prose, and personal reflections from Rod to Heron Dancers. The following 5 pages contain samples of our *Pause for Beauty* newsletters. To sign up, please visit our website: www.herondance.org.

My goal is to live the truly religious life and express it in my music.

        John Coltrane

After reviewing and reliving John Coltrane's incredibly brave career and his burning musical curiosity, which was tied to a desire to know God and the very rhythms of the cosmos, it is especially hard not to be put off by such reactionary music and aesthetics. Wynton Marsalis is becoming a better player every time I hear him, and now there is beginning to be heard some real emotional resonance in his playing. Yet there is something missing, and it is missing in just about all of those neoclassicists that I have heard. Miles would call it "that thing," and it has much to do with the chances we must take in life in order for our souls to survive.

       Eric Nisenson from *Ascension: John Coltrane and His Quest*

January 1

Today carve out a quiet interlude for yourself in which to dream, pen in hand. Only dreams give birth to change. [...]. Believe in yourself. And believe that there is a loving Source — A Sower of Dreams — just waiting to be asked to help you make your dreams come true.

January 2

What if you knew that a year from today you could be living the most creative, joyous, and fulfilling life you could imagine? What would it be? What changes would you make?

January 7

What is missing from many of our days is a true sense that we are enjoying the lives we are living. It is difficult to experience moments of happiness if we are not aware of what it is we genuinely love. We must learn to savor small, authentic moments that bring us contentment.

Sarah Ban Breathnach from *Simple Abundance: A Daybook of Comfort and Joy*

Spring is in the air. The breeze is gentle with the smell of birthing, the earth radiates freshness, the birds sing with more abandon than they have for months. The first wildflowers are in bloom in the deep forest: the hardy toothwort, the delicate purple shooting star. The tender green of new growth is everywhere.

Barbara Dean from *Wellspring*

Aug. 4, 6 P.M.—Lights and shades and rare effects on tree-foliage and grass—transparent greens, grays, &c., all in sunset pomp and dazzle. The clear beams are now thrown in many new places, on the quilted, seam'd, bronze-drab, lower tree-trunks, shadow'd except at this hour—now flooding their young and old columnar ruggedness with strong light, unfolding to my sense new amazing features of silent, shaggy charm, the solid bark, the expression of harmless impassiveness, with many a bulge and gnarl unreck'd before. In the revealings of such light, such exceptional hour, such mood, one does not wonder at the old story fables, (indeed, why fables?) of people falling into love-sickness with trees, seiz'd extatic [sic] with the mystic realism of the resistless silent strength in them—*strength*, which after all is perhaps the last, completest, highest beauty.

Walt Whitman from *The Lesson of a Tree*

Those who have drunk lonesome water are not in their right minds. It's more than loving the land. It seems for me the thing for which you spend your whole life to build, if you would be whole, is not a bank account, or an unimpeachable social position, or success in any one of a thousand lines of endeavor; it seems to me that the only thing worth having is a certainty of yourself. People who have this knowledge are people who have kept their edges intact, people with what I can only call core; by which I mean the indestructible skeleton of character, showing through manner and mannerism, as good bones show through flesh. It's one thing you know you can count on in yourself and in others, and it's not easily acquired.

Louise Dickinson Rich from *Happy The Land*

HERON DANCE art by Roderick MacIver

Most of the paintings found in this book are available
as limited-edition prints at www.herondance.org.

Heron Dance is a Work of Love

Founded in 1995 by artist Roderick MacIver, Heron Dance is a celebration of life and of the beauty and mystery of the natural world. Supported by donations and the sale of art and books, Heron Dance strives to provide a respite in this fast-paced world.

Wild Nature Paintings by Roderick MacIver

Hundreds of images are available as limited-edition prints, originals, and notecards. Please visit our website to view: www.herondance.org.

Heron Dance Publication

Heron Dance is a full-color journal featuring the wild nature paintings of Roderick MacIver, and essays, interviews, poetry, and quotations that explore the human search for meaning and the human connection to the natural world.

To learn more, please visit our website, www.herondance.org.

A Pause for Beauty

This free, weekly email features Roderick MacIver's latest wild nature painting and a poem, quotation or other reflection. To sign up, visit www.herondance.org.

Online Studio Store (see our website)

We offer notecards, daybooks, calendars, address books, and both blank and inspirational journals that feature Roderick MacIver's wild nature paintings. Additionally, Heron Dance carries a selection of thought-provoking books, including *The Man Who Planted Trees, Thoreau and the Art of Life,* and *Meditations on Nature, Meditations on Silence.*

Nonprofit Donations

Each year, Heron Dance donates thousands of notecards and the use of images to small, nonprofit wilderness protection groups, including The Northeast Wilderness Trust: www.newildernesstrust.org.

www.herondance.org

In addition to offering Roderick MacIver's wild nature paintings, the *Heron Dance* publication, the free weekly newsletter (*A Pause for Beauty*), and other Heron Dance products, the Heron Dance website is filled with inspirational interviews, essays, book excerpts, and poetry.

ALSO FROM HERON DANCE
All titles feature Roderick MacIver Wild Nature Paintings

Art as a Way of Life

This beautiful and inspiring book helps us to discover and nurture the creative spirit that is within us all. Filled with Roderick MacIver's unique nature paintings, Annie O'Shaughnessy's short reflections, and selections from many other creative voices, *Art as a Way of Life* is a truly empowering and encouraging book for people wanting to live, work, and love in the creative spirit. 96 pages.

#6093 *Art as a Way of Life* — $12.95

Meditations on Nature, Meditations on Silence

Through paintings, poetry, and excerpts from books and interviews, *Meditations on Nature, Meditations on Silence* explores the beauty, strange cohesion, and complexity of the natural world and universe. It offers readers a retreat from our complex, fast-paced world. This book is a follow-up to our very popular *Heron Dance Book of Love and Gratitude*. 96 pages.

#6090 *Meditations on Nature, Meditations on Silence* — $12.95

Pausing for Beauty: The Heron Dance Poetry Diary

We designed this diary just as we wanted it — with plenty of inspiring poetry and art AND plenty of blank and lined pages. Containing over 140 of Roderick's nature paintings, the diary also has 12 full-page, dateless calendars, one at the start of every month, so the book can be used for any year. 176 pages.

#1606 *Pausing for Beauty: The Heron Dance Poetry Diary* — $17.95

Love and Gratitude Notecard Set

Each of the five cards in this assortment features a different quotation chosen from *The Heron Dance Book of Love and Gratitude,* along with one of Roderick's beautiful nature paintings. Sized a bit smaller than our other notecards at 5.5" x 4.25", these cards are perfect for a quick thank you or note of encouragement. Each set has 10 blank cards and 11 envelopes.

1404LG   *Love and Gratitude Notecards* — $12.95

Heron Dance offers over a dozen notecards. Some have simple one-color washes with an inspirational quote, while others feature the rich tones of Roderick MacIver's wild nature watercolors and come greeted or blank. Our holiday cards have been especially popular. Please visit the Studio Store section of our website for more information.